My Positive Moments Journal
a workbook companion to warm your days

Jerald R Forster, PhD
and
Jennifer L Rose, MA, CYT500

ArticulatingYourStrengths.org
Seattle, WA

© 2024 Jerald R Forster and Jennifer L Rose
All Rights Reserved
For more Information: ArticulatingYourStrengths.org

ISBN: 979-8-218-43642-1

Do not reproduce without permission.

Visit www.amazon.com to order additional copies.

Cover photo © Jennifer L Rose

My Positive Moments Journal

Focus your attention on internal positivity.

By regularly writing down positive moments you are building a habit of paying more attention to your positive feelings. "Positive feelings" happen when you feel good (even for very brief moments, such as seeing someone smile or settling into a deep, calm breath). You are learning more about what makes you feel good. This is an experiential way of learning about what makes life worth living for you.

Writing about positive moments helps you bring them more clearly into focus and remember them. At the beginning, you may need a structure to build your attention to positivity. This journal provides that structure.

The idea is to record positive moments regularly, so you begin to notice that positive moments are occurring all the time. Consider setting a timer to ring three times a day to remind you to write a positive moment in this journal. When it's time to write, notice: How are you feeling now? What was the most satisfying moment you experienced recently? Write about that moment whether it is big or small. Another way to remind yourself to use your journal is to place it in a location where you will regularly see it, such as on your work desk. You could also record moments on your phone or in a pocket-size notebook that you would later transfer to this journal.

Suppose your mind suggests, "There hasn't been a positive moment." Challenge this. Surely one moment stands out a bit from the others. You are more likely to capture these moments if you are regular about writing in your journal throughout the day. This is why we created pages with sections for morning, afternoon, and evening. With practice, noticing positive moments comes more easily. Focus on your feelings, that is what guides your writing here. Be as specific as you can be about the moment that felt the best, whether it makes sense or not, whether someone else might understand it or not doesn't matter. Trust your feelings, and you will be able to learn from paying attention to what feels good to you. Do your best to record what happened in the positive moment and what it felt like. This will give you material to reflect on with regard to what you value and what you enjoy.

If you share your journal entries with another person, it will amplify your own positivity, and the other person might get more positive ideas and notice positive moments like yours and vice versa. Sharing will also give you a chance to reflect further on what your positive moments are teaching you about yourself. For this reason, we suggest inviting someone to join you in this journaling experience. You can share your journal entries in person or online. In time, you will evolve a new kind of relationship with this person/people. Your appreciation for their positivity and how they express it grows and grows, especially if you meet regularly, such as once a week, for a long time.

When you want to develop your positivity practice further, check out the free resources at ArticulatingYourStrengths.org. Here, you can find video instruction that will help you describe your strengths and your positive identity using the Strengths-focused Identity Practice (SfI-Practice). Focusing on your positive identity helps you feel that the things you like about yourself describe who you really are.

The SfI-Practice strives to help an individual practitioner become more aware of, and more articulate in describing, what he/she/they are currently thinking and feeling at the very moment it is happening.

The better you get at articulating your processing of what is happening in the present moment, the better you will become at deciding whether or not you will continue with, or change, what is happening internally. The individual who is aware of what is happening at the present moment will be able to change what is happening more quickly, which will enable you to experience more positive thoughts/feelings than you would have if you had not gained this new ability/skill.

Becoming more proficient in this SfI-Practice will permit you to increase the amount of time each day when you are feeling good. Over your lifetime, this will enable you to experience much more happiness and satisfaction than you would otherwise have experienced. Can you think of anything more important than that?

On the next pages, you will find examples of how to write in your journal and some feeling words to help you if you get stuck naming your positive feelings.

Two examples of writing a positive moment in your journal:

Example 1

Morning
What happened? Which part of the experience really felt good? How did I feel?

I really liked the ham and eggs I had for breakfast this morning.

I felt satisfied with the flavors and the experience of eating. I get a joy out of watching the ham and eggs cook through the glass lid. I can tell when the eggs are done perfectly. With a little salt, it's a nice flavor to savor.

Example 2

Evening
What happened? Which part of the experience really felt good? How did I feel?

During my grade 4 writing class, my student R. volunteered to read aloud "Turtle Soup" by Lewis Carroll. When he pronounced the line "Beau–ootiful Soo–oop!" again and again, it eventually really gave him a belly laugh.

Seeing his big, happy smile and hearing his happy laughter made me feel both pure glee and some success at giving a student a meaningful connection to poetry.

Positive Feeling Words and Phrases

Have fun adding your own words to the list on the next page.

Peaceful Feelings approving, at ease, calm, cherished / cherishing, comfortable, content, expansive, faithful, glad, god- conscious, harmonious, moved, placid, protected, quiet, relaxed, safe, satisfied, secure, self- accepting, still, treasured / treasuring	**Joyful Feelings** beatific, blissful, bright, cheerful, delighted, divine, ecstatic, elated, enriched, exhilarated, exultant, euphoric, fervent, happy, hopeful, inspired, motivated, optimistic, positive, resplendent, stirred, transcendent, unlimited, uplifted
Loving Feelings accepted / accepting, adored / adoring, admired / admiring, appreciated / appreciative, befriended, celebratory, connected, close, delighted in / delighting in, encouraged / encouraging, forgiven / forgiving, generous, giving, grateful, nurtured / nurturing, open, protected / protective, respected / respecting, sustained, thankful, trusted / trusting, understood / understanding	**Feelings of Empowerment** accomplished, artistic, certain, creative, dignified, energetic, expert, fulfilled, gratified, healthy, honored, important, informed, indispensable, intelligent, knowledgeable, learned, nourished, informed, inventive, original, pleased, proud, recognized, rewarded, successful, valued / valuable, worthy
Wise Feelings absorbed, alert, astute, attuned, aware, centered, discerning, focused, free, insightful, introspective, intuitive, judicious, liberated, one- pointed, open, perceptive, sensitive, unbound, unfettered, wise	**Exciting Feelings** amazed, awed, brave, curious, courageous, daring, engaged, enthusiastic, fearless, frisky, funny, hilarious, interested, intrigued, laughing, lively, on- fire, passionate, reverent, spirited, stimulated

Finding your own words is an important part of this process. Your positive experiences are completely unique. You are likely to evolve your own way of talking about them. As you practice, your attention to your feeling states becomes more acute. You will develop language to match your evolving observations about your feelings over time.

My Own Positive Feeling Words:

My Positive Moments Journal

Morning
What happened? Which part of the experience really felt good? How did I feel?

Afternoon
What happened? Which part of the experience really felt good? How did I feel?

Evening
What happened? Which part of the experience really felt good? How did I feel?

Morning
What happened? Which part of the experience really felt good? How did I feel?

Afternoon
What happened? Which part of the experience really felt good? How did I feel?

Evening
What happened? Which part of the experience really felt good? How did I feel?

Morning
What happened? Which part of the experience really felt good? How did I feel?

Afternoon
What happened? Which part of the experience really felt good? How did I feel?

Evening
What happened? Which part of the experience really felt good? How did I feel?

Morning

What happened? Which part of the experience really felt good? How did I feel?

Afternoon

What happened? Which part of the experience really felt good? How did I feel?

Evening

What happened? Which part of the experience really felt good? How did I feel?

Morning
What happened? Which part of the experience really felt good? How did I feel?

Afternoon
What happened? Which part of the experience really felt good? How did I feel?

Evening
What happened? Which part of the experience really felt good? How did I feel?

Morning
What happened? Which part of the experience really felt good? How did I feel?

Afternoon
What happened? Which part of the experience really felt good? How did I feel?

Evening
What happened? Which part of the experience really felt good? How did I feel?

Morning
What happened? Which part of the experience really felt good? How did I feel?

Afternoon
What happened? Which part of the experience really felt good? How did I feel?

Evening
What happened? Which part of the experience really felt good? How did I feel?

Congratulations! You have recorded a week of positive moments. That is 21 positive moments. It's time to give yourself a pat on the back. You might enjoy looking back on what you have recorded so far. Reviewing your positive moments can be a source of inspiration for creating opportunities for those kinds of moments in the present or the future.

Whatever lifts the corners of the mouth, trust that.
—Rumi, 12th Century

Keep up the good work. You have started a practice that is going to change your life.

Morning
What happened? Which part of the experience really felt good? How did I feel?

Afternoon
What happened? Which part of the experience really felt good? How did I feel?

Evening
What happened? Which part of the experience really felt good? How did I feel?

Morning
What happened? Which part of the experience really felt good? How did I feel?

Afternoon
What happened? Which part of the experience really felt good? How did I feel?

Evening
What happened? Which part of the experience really felt good? How did I feel?

Morning
What happened? Which part of the experience really felt good? How did I feel?

Afternoon
What happened? Which part of the experience really felt good? How did I feel?

Evening
What happened? Which part of the experience really felt good? How did I feel?

Morning
What happened? Which part of the experience really felt good? How did I feel?

Afternoon
What happened? Which part of the experience really felt good? How did I feel?

Evening
What happened? Which part of the experience really felt good? How did I feel?

Morning
What happened? Which part of the experience really felt good? How did I feel?

Afternoon
What happened? Which part of the experience really felt good? How did I feel?

Evening
What happened? Which part of the experience really felt good? How did I feel?

Morning
What happened? Which part of the experience really felt good? How did I feel?

Afternoon
What happened? Which part of the experience really felt good? How did I feel?

Evening
What happened? Which part of the experience really felt good? How did I feel?

Morning
What happened? Which part of the experience really felt good? How did I feel?

Afternoon
What happened? Which part of the experience really felt good? How did I feel?

Evening
What happened? Which part of the experience really felt good? How did I feel?

Well done! Now you have recorded two weeks of positive moments. Is it starting to seem clear that life is a mix of emotions? There are many positive ones to notice every day. As you keep practicing you will notice more and more different kinds of positive feelings.

Each day provides its own gifts.
–Marcus Aurelieus 2nd Century

If you want to mix it up this week, use the list of positive feelings at the beginning of the journal to expand your ideas about what is positive. Challenge yourself to record some new kinds of positive experiences and related positive feelings this week.

Morning

What happened? Which part of the experience really felt good? How did I feel?

Afternoon

What happened? Which part of the experience really felt good? How did I feel?

Evening

What happened? Which part of the experience really felt good? How did I feel?

Morning
What happened? Which part of the experience really felt good? How did I feel?

Afternoon
What happened? Which part of the experience really felt good? How did I feel?

Evening
What happened? Which part of the experience really felt good? How did I feel?

Morning

What happened? Which part of the experience really felt good? How did I feel?

Afternoon

What happened? Which part of the experience really felt good? How did I feel?

Evening

What happened? Which part of the experience really felt good? How did I feel?

Morning
What happened? Which part of the experience really felt good? How did I feel?

Afternoon
What happened? Which part of the experience really felt good? How did I feel?

Evening
What happened? Which part of the experience really felt good? How did I feel?

Morning
What happened? Which part of the experience really felt good? How did I feel?

Afternoon
What happened? Which part of the experience really felt good? How did I feel?

Evening
What happened? Which part of the experience really felt good? How did I feel?

Morning
What happened? Which part of the experience really felt good? How did I feel?

Afternoon
What happened? Which part of the experience really felt good? How did I feel?

Evening
What happened? Which part of the experience really felt good? How did I feel?

Morning

What happened? Which part of the experience really felt good? How did I feel?

Afternoon

What happened? Which part of the experience really felt good? How did I feel?

Evening

What happened? Which part of the experience really felt good? How did I feel?

Congratulations on recording three weeks of positive moments. 63 positive moments! That is a lot of good feelings. (You may be recording more or fewer, and that is okay. We just want you to recognize what you have accomplished.) When we experience positive feelings, those feelings are attributes of ourselves, not attributes of outside events or things. By articulating positive moments, you are becoming your best self.

Keep your thoughts positive because your thoughts become your words. Keep your words positive because your words become your behavior. Keep your behavior positive because your behavior becomes your habits. Keep your habits positive because your habits become your values. Keep your values positive because your values become your destiny.
–Mahatma Gandhi

If you want a cue to regularly record positive moments, try tying it to your meals, right before or right after you eat. You could also place sticky-note reminders in places you see regularly. Or try carrying a small notebook with you, so you don't have to return to your journal to write your positive moment. You can transfer it to your journal later from your notebook or phone.

The greatest help in being regular will be to record every day at the same time. If you look at your schedule and figure out the right time for you, that will make all the difference. Plan when you will do your positive moments writing ahead of time, or it may not get done.

Here is an example schedule:
1. after breakfast
2. before lunch
3. around 4:00 in afternoon

You should be flexible with yourself. Modify your schedule as needed overall, as well as to respond to the needs of each day. The point of the planning is not to be rigid. The point is that planning increases the likelihood of recalling and writing down your most positive moments.

If you get really good at recording your *most* positive moments, expand your positivity horizons by recording novel positive moments. More and more, you will learn to notice what is positive *now*.

Morning

What happened? Which part of the experience really felt good? How did I feel?

Afternoon

What happened? Which part of the experience really felt good? How did I feel?

Evening

What happened? Which part of the experience really felt good? How did I feel?

Morning
What happened? Which part of the experience really felt good? How did I feel?

Afternoon
What happened? Which part of the experience really felt good? How did I feel?

Evening
What happened? Which part of the experience really felt good? How did I feel?

Morning
What happened? Which part of the experience really felt good? How did I feel?

Afternoon
What happened? Which part of the experience really felt good? How did I feel?

Evening
What happened? Which part of the experience really felt good? How did I feel?

Morning
What happened? Which part of the experience really felt good? How did I feel?

Afternoon
What happened? Which part of the experience really felt good? How did I feel?

Evening
What happened? Which part of the experience really felt good? How did I feel?

Morning

What happened? Which part of the experience really felt good? How did I feel?

Afternoon

What happened? Which part of the experience really felt good? How did I feel?

Evening

What happened? Which part of the experience really felt good? How did I feel?

Morning
What happened? Which part of the experience really felt good? How did I feel?

Afternoon
What happened? Which part of the experience really felt good? How did I feel?

Evening
What happened? Which part of the experience really felt good? How did I feel?

Morning

What happened? Which part of the experience really felt good? How did I feel?

Afternoon

What happened? Which part of the experience really felt good? How did I feel?

Evening

What happened? Which part of the experience really felt good? How did I feel?

4 weeks of positive moments. Good for you. Your practice is becoming internalized. That means you find yourself doing it in your mind throughout the day. Maybe there are times during your day, such as making breakfast, that you have noticed are always somewhat positive. These times can become daily opportunities for you to experience positivity. What if you developed many of these habits throughout your day?

Taking delight in my family, my time in nature, and in the chance to do work that I find endlessly fascinating and rewarding. My smile grows even bigger when I think about how lucky I am to have such delights be part of my everyday life.

–Barbara Fredrickson, positive psychology pioneer, in response to this interview question: What makes you smile inside and out, and why?

This week, try to record at least one positive moment that is part of your daily routine.

Morning
What happened? Which part of the experience really felt good? How did I feel?

Afternoon
What happened? Which part of the experience really felt good? How did I feel?

Evening
What happened? Which part of the experience really felt good? How did I feel?

Morning
What happened? Which part of the experience really felt good? How did I feel?

Afternoon
What happened? Which part of the experience really felt good? How did I feel?

Evening
What happened? Which part of the experience really felt good? How did I feel?

Morning

What happened? Which part of the experience really felt good? How did I feel?

Afternoon

What happened? Which part of the experience really felt good? How did I feel?

Evening

What happened? Which part of the experience really felt good? How did I feel?

Morning
What happened? Which part of the experience really felt good? How did I feel?

Afternoon
What happened? Which part of the experience really felt good? How did I feel?

Evening
What happened? Which part of the experience really felt good? How did I feel?

Morning

What happened? Which part of the experience really felt good? How did I feel?

Afternoon

What happened? Which part of the experience really felt good? How did I feel?

Evening

What happened? Which part of the experience really felt good? How did I feel?

Morning
What happened? Which part of the experience really felt good? How did I feel?

Afternoon
What happened? Which part of the experience really felt good? How did I feel?

Evening
What happened? Which part of the experience really felt good? How did I feel?

Morning
What happened? Which part of the experience really felt good? How did I feel?

Afternoon
What happened? Which part of the experience really felt good? How did I feel?

Evening
What happened? Which part of the experience really felt good? How did I feel?

You have completed 5 weeks! Way to go! Have you established a habit of reflecting on positive moments three times per day? It's okay if you haven't established that habit yet, but we want to encourage you to keep that as a goal. We have noticed that recording positive moments three times per day increases our attention to positivity at times of the day when we might be less likely to notice it. For example, what is positive "at work"? If we have an anxious or put-out orientation to work, we might skip that part of the day for recording positive moments, but that would be a lot of little positive moments that go unnoticed and unappreciated.

Knowing that we will be recording a positive moment for a particular part of the day changes how we attend to what is happening. Then, when positivity is observed, the potential arises for it to be repeated. Times of day that had previously been obscured by negative connotations can become more positive.

Optimism is a strategy for making a better future. Because unless you believe that the future can be better, you are unlikely to step up and take responsibility for making it so.

–Noam Chomsky

By articulating positive moments, you are changing your present and affecting your future. You are making them both more positive. See if you can notice how the practice creates changes in how you experience your upcoming week.

Morning
What happened? Which part of the experience really felt good? How did I feel?

Afternoon
What happened? Which part of the experience really felt good? How did I feel?

Evening
What happened? Which part of the experience really felt good? How did I feel?

Morning

What happened? Which part of the experience really felt good? How did I feel?

Afternoon

What happened? Which part of the experience really felt good? How did I feel?

Evening

What happened? Which part of the experience really felt good? How did I feel?

Morning
What happened? Which part of the experience really felt good? How did I feel?

Afternoon
What happened? Which part of the experience really felt good? How did I feel?

Evening
What happened? Which part of the experience really felt good? How did I feel?

Morning
What happened? Which part of the experience really felt good? How did I feel?

Afternoon
What happened? Which part of the experience really felt good? How did I feel?

Evening
What happened? Which part of the experience really felt good? How did I feel?

Morning
What happened? Which part of the experience really felt good? How did I feel?

Afternoon
What happened? Which part of the experience really felt good? How did I feel?

Evening
What happened? Which part of the experience really felt good? How did I feel?

Morning

What happened? Which part of the experience really felt good? How did I feel?

Afternoon

What happened? Which part of the experience really felt good? How did I feel?

Evening

What happened? Which part of the experience really felt good? How did I feel?

Morning
What happened? Which part of the experience really felt good? How did I feel?

Afternoon
What happened? Which part of the experience really felt good? How did I feel?

Evening
What happened? Which part of the experience really felt good? How did I feel?

Here's a strategy for reminding yourself to record your positive moments. In places where you will typically spend time in the morning, afternoon, and evening, place sticky notes that say, "Record a positive moment." That will help you pause for the short time it takes to write down something recent that made you feel a bit better than you usually feel. For example, if you spend a lot of time on your computer in the afternoon, you could put a sticky note there. If you have a routine of eating something in the morning, you could have a sticky note on your refrigerator.

> *While we may not be able to control all that happens to us,*
> *we can control what happens inside us.*
> –Benjamin Franklin

For some, it is difficult to believe we can control what happens inside us, or that it would be a good thing to do. Although negativity may come automatically, positivity can be increased if we do it intentionally. It is perfectly normal to have negative thoughts, partly because of the negativity bias that may have once helped us survive. However, it is not *necessary* to have these thoughts, and we do not have to persist in them. We can make positive efforts to have a more positive mental outlook.

This week, try to transform a negative moment into a positive one by changing your thoughts about what is happening. For example, if you notice yourself perseverating on something negative, intentionally switch to thoughts of gratitude. You can be grateful for circumstances, relationships, life itself, or any other thing. This technique has been studied and determined to be effective.

Morning

What happened? Which part of the experience really felt good? How did I feel?

Afternoon

What happened? Which part of the experience really felt good? How did I feel?

Evening

What happened? Which part of the experience really felt good? How did I feel?

Morning

What happened? Which part of the experience really felt good? How did I feel?

Afternoon

What happened? Which part of the experience really felt good? How did I feel?

Evening

What happened? Which part of the experience really felt good? How did I feel?

Morning
What happened? Which part of the experience really felt good? How did I feel?

Afternoon
What happened? Which part of the experience really felt good? How did I feel?

Evening
What happened? Which part of the experience really felt good? How did I feel?

Morning

What happened? Which part of the experience really felt good? How did I feel?

Afternoon

What happened? Which part of the experience really felt good? How did I feel?

Evening

What happened? Which part of the experience really felt good? How did I feel?

Morning
What happened? Which part of the experience really felt good? How did I feel?

Afternoon
What happened? Which part of the experience really felt good? How did I feel?

Evening
What happened? Which part of the experience really felt good? How did I feel?

Morning
What happened? Which part of the experience really felt good? How did I feel?

Afternoon
What happened? Which part of the experience really felt good? How did I feel?

Evening
What happened? Which part of the experience really felt good? How did I feel?

Morning
What happened? Which part of the experience really felt good? How did I feel?

Afternoon
What happened? Which part of the experience really felt good? How did I feel?

Evening
What happened? Which part of the experience really felt good? How did I feel?

Congratulations! You have recorded 7 weeks of positive moments. That is 147 positive moments. Recording them this way makes them indisputably real. Sometimes, our negativity makes generalizations such as, *I'm always feeling sad*. You can counter such thoughts by rereading your positive moments. It is likely to make you feel better and prepare you for more positive moments.

> *"Martin Seligman, the director of the Positive Psychology Center at the University of Pennsylvania, recommends an easy ritual: Every evening for one week, write down three things that went well that day, and why. The goal is to train your attention away from the bad things in life and focus on the good things."*
>
> Dana G. Smith, *"How Are You Really?"* New York Times, March 5, 2024

We recommend that you do the practice throughout the day and over a longer period of time to have a more profound transformative effect, but our idea is basically the same as Seligman's. Doing the practice more regularly invites you to consider smaller, more subtle positive moments. Here's something to try this week: When we have happy anticipation of an upcoming event, feeling that anticipation is a positive moment. For example, looking ahead to seeing someone you enjoy being with is often a positive moment. See if you can record one or more of these moments of happy anticipation this week.

Morning
What happened? Which part of the experience really felt good? How did I feel?

Afternoon
What happened? Which part of the experience really felt good? How did I feel?

Evening
What happened? Which part of the experience really felt good? How did I feel?

Morning
What happened? Which part of the experience really felt good? How did I feel?

Afternoon
What happened? Which part of the experience really felt good? How did I feel?

Evening
What happened? Which part of the experience really felt good? How did I feel?

Morning
What happened? Which part of the experience really felt good? How did I feel?

Afternoon
What happened? Which part of the experience really felt good? How did I feel?

Evening
What happened? Which part of the experience really felt good? How did I feel?

Morning
What happened? Which part of the experience really felt good? How did I feel?

Afternoon
What happened? Which part of the experience really felt good? How did I feel?

Evening
What happened? Which part of the experience really felt good? How did I feel?

Morning
What happened? Which part of the experience really felt good? How did I feel?

Afternoon
What happened? Which part of the experience really felt good? How did I feel?

Evening
What happened? Which part of the experience really felt good? How did I feel?

Morning

What happened? Which part of the experience really felt good? How did I feel?

Afternoon

What happened? Which part of the experience really felt good? How did I feel?

Evening

What happened? Which part of the experience really felt good? How did I feel?

Morning
What happened? Which part of the experience really felt good? How did I feel?

Afternoon
What happened? Which part of the experience really felt good? How did I feel?

Evening
What happened? Which part of the experience really felt good? How did I feel?

Now, you have recorded 8 weeks of positive moments. As you become more aware of what makes you feel positive, you can reflect and elaborate on those things more often. You have more content within you that you can recall when things go wrong, and this will interrupt perseveration and clear your mind.

Everything can be taken from a man but one thing: the last of the human freedoms—to choose one's attitude in any given set of circumstances, to choose one's own way. When we are no longer able to change a situation, we are challenged to change ourselves.

–Viktor Frankl

Some positive moments are related to external events, but some are completely internal. Feelings of success, accomplishment, appreciation, love and many others can be extended in time by a psychological process called *savoring*. Viktor Frankl was in a Nazi concentration camp when he conceived the quote above. On a brutal march through the snow while guards whipped and verbally abused him and other prisoners, Frankl realized that no one could stop him from thinking lovingly about his wife, and that would create for him an internal positive moment. Could you record an internal positive moment that takes place during circumstances that other people might describe as negative?

Morning
What happened? Which part of the experience really felt good? How did I feel?

Afternoon
What happened? Which part of the experience really felt good? How did I feel?

Evening
What happened? Which part of the experience really felt good? How did I feel?

Morning
What happened? Which part of the experience really felt good? How did I feel?

Afternoon
What happened? Which part of the experience really felt good? How did I feel?

Evening
What happened? Which part of the experience really felt good? How did I feel?

Morning
What happened? Which part of the experience really felt good? How did I feel?

Afternoon
What happened? Which part of the experience really felt good? How did I feel?

Evening
What happened? Which part of the experience really felt good? How did I feel?

Morning
What happened? Which part of the experience really felt good? How did I feel?

Afternoon
What happened? Which part of the experience really felt good? How did I feel?

Evening
What happened? Which part of the experience really felt good? How did I feel?

Morning
What happened? Which part of the experience really felt good? How did I feel?

Afternoon
What happened? Which part of the experience really felt good? How did I feel?

Evening
What happened? Which part of the experience really felt good? How did I feel?

Morning

What happened? Which part of the experience really felt good? How did I feel?

Afternoon

What happened? Which part of the experience really felt good? How did I feel?

Evening

What happened? Which part of the experience really felt good? How did I feel?

Morning
What happened? Which part of the experience really felt good? How did I feel?

Afternoon
What happened? Which part of the experience really felt good? How did I feel?

Evening
What happened? Which part of the experience really felt good? How did I feel?

9 weeks and 186 positive moments. Good for you! Practicing has probably made you more aware of your positive feelings as they are happening in the present moment. If you are bringing attention to your positive feelings in the moment, you might start to notice that you feel them more intensely. There is an idea that what we give our attention to is magnified. If we pay attention to our suffering, it is magnified. If we pay attention to our positive feelings, they are magnified.

You must live in the present, launch yourself on every wave, find your eternity in each moment. Fools stand on their island of opportunities and look toward another land. There is no other land; there is no other life but this.

– Henry David Thoreau

This week, try to notice and record a few positive moments right in the moment that they are happening, or very shortly afterward.

Morning

What happened? Which part of the experience really felt good? How did I feel?

Afternoon

What happened? Which part of the experience really felt good? How did I feel?

Evening

What happened? Which part of the experience really felt good? How did I feel?

Morning
What happened? Which part of the experience really felt good? How did I feel?

Afternoon
What happened? Which part of the experience really felt good? How did I feel?

Evening
What happened? Which part of the experience really felt good? How did I feel?

Morning
What happened? Which part of the experience really felt good? How did I feel?

Afternoon
What happened? Which part of the experience really felt good? How did I feel?

Evening
What happened? Which part of the experience really felt good? How did I feel?

Morning

What happened? Which part of the experience really felt good? How did I feel?

Afternoon

What happened? Which part of the experience really felt good? How did I feel?

Evening

What happened? Which part of the experience really felt good? How did I feel?

Morning

What happened? Which part of the experience really felt good? How did I feel?

Afternoon

What happened? Which part of the experience really felt good? How did I feel?

Evening

What happened? Which part of the experience really felt good? How did I feel?

Morning

What happened? Which part of the experience really felt good? How did I feel?

Afternoon

What happened? Which part of the experience really felt good? How did I feel?

Evening

What happened? Which part of the experience really felt good? How did I feel?

Morning
What happened? Which part of the experience really felt good? How did I feel?

Afternoon
What happened? Which part of the experience really felt good? How did I feel?

Evening
What happened? Which part of the experience really felt good? How did I feel?

Ten weeks, 210 positive moments. That is a lot of positivity. Have you noticed any changes in your experiences?

Human beings, by changing the inner attitudes of their minds, can change the outer aspects of their lives."

– William James, psychologist, philosopher

This week, try this challenge. Is there something in your life that you typically associate with negativity? Can you find something positive in it? Here is an example: Reading the newspaper can be associated with helpless, sad or angry feelings. However, some people find the sports section to be positive or find the science stories to be inspiring. Try to refocus a negative experience by directing attention to a positive part of it.

Morning
What happened? Which part of the experience really felt good? How did I feel?

Afternoon
What happened? Which part of the experience really felt good? How did I feel?

Evening
What happened? Which part of the experience really felt good? How did I feel?

Morning

What happened? Which part of the experience really felt good? How did I feel?

Afternoon

What happened? Which part of the experience really felt good? How did I feel?

Evening

What happened? Which part of the experience really felt good? How did I feel?

Morning

What happened? Which part of the experience really felt good? How did I feel?

Afternoon

What happened? Which part of the experience really felt good? How did I feel?

Evening

What happened? Which part of the experience really felt good? How did I feel?

Morning
What happened? Which part of the experience really felt good? How did I feel?

Afternoon
What happened? Which part of the experience really felt good? How did I feel?

Evening
What happened? Which part of the experience really felt good? How did I feel?

Morning

What happened? Which part of the experience really felt good? How did I feel?

Afternoon

What happened? Which part of the experience really felt good? How did I feel?

Evening

What happened? Which part of the experience really felt good? How did I feel?

Morning

What happened? Which part of the experience really felt good? How did I feel?

Afternoon

What happened? Which part of the experience really felt good? How did I feel?

Evening

What happened? Which part of the experience really felt good? How did I feel?

Morning
What happened? Which part of the experience really felt good? How did I feel?

Afternoon
What happened? Which part of the experience really felt good? How did I feel?

Evening
What happened? Which part of the experience really felt good? How did I feel?

By now, you have hundreds of positive moments written down. We want to give you an idea of how to develop these moments (although we want you to keep recording positive moments, and you will find one more page for recording positive moments on the last page of the book that you can copy so you never run out. You can also find a downloadable page on our website:
https://articulatingyourstrengths.org/index.php/beginning-sfi-practice-lesson-4/).

In addition, the website, ArticulatingYourStrengths.org, has extensive instructions in the Strengths-focused Identity Practice. It has examples that show how to build a positive identity starting from positive moments.

It is not *necessary* to go any further with the practice than the recording of positive moments. You can elevate your positivity just with the simple practice in this workbook. However, there is a way to build on your awareness of your positive moments to also become aware of positive qualities you have. To that end, we would like to make a parting gift of a method of gaining clarity about what you like about yourself.

Strengths articulation is a method for building your positive self identity. In addition to drawing awareness to positive moments, having positive ideas about yourself is a way of feeling better overall. It can make you self-reliant and help you be resilient when you experience losses, the negative judgments of others, or other disruptions to your positivity. It helps you communicate the best part of yourself to others. This facilitates interactions and relationships in which others engage with the best parts of your personality. Positive relationships and interactions create the kind of society we all want to be part of.

How can you use your positive moments to lead to insights into what you like about yourself? The root idea is that you are always a part of your positive moments. You are not just enjoying them, you are also creating them through your strengths, also known as your positive qualities. So, by being aware of and analyzing your positive moments you can discover your best qualities. By "best qualities" we mean those qualities that result in positive moments. We do not mean those qualities that other people or society makes the most use of or values the most. It is all based on what makes you feel positive in your life.

You are born to be content and happy with yourself. You may be a very skilled bookkeeper, but if that does not make you happy, it is not the kind of strength we are talking about here. If it does make you happy, then it absolutely is the kind of strength we are talking about. A "strength" in our way of looking at it, is something you use and feel stronger and more energetic for using it. It is not something that depletes you by using it. Strengths should be strengthening for you, not depleting.

Here are two examples of how to use your positive moments to investigate your strengths. Choose some of the positive moments you have recorded in this workbook. Then, spend some time speculating about your own attributes that play a part in creating those positive moments.

Example 1:

List a few positive moments:

1 Making breakfast.

2 Reading the newspaper, especially the sports page.

3 Having regular Zoom conversations with someone.

My ideas about strengths that might have contributed to making these moments possible:

Doing my best with everyday activities, and giving them my full attention
Organization
Planning
Feeling positive most of time
Feeling fortunate/grateful
Directing attention to positive experiences, thoughts, and feelings most of the time
Prioritizing my life so I have time and space for activities I value
Open to new ideas
Good conversationalist
Psychological growth mindset

Example 2:

List a few positive moments:

1 Doing the crossword puzzle with Kendall

2 Writing a poem at the cafe

3 Walking in the rhododendron garden

My ideas about strengths that might have contributed to making these moments possible:

linguistic intelligence
teamwork
stick-to-itiveness
facility with language
contemplative
attentive
nature lover

It may take a while to get comfortable with articulating your strengths. If that is the case, you can use this list of strengths words to help you. Later, you will likely feel more comfortable coming up with your own words and phrases. Your own words and phrases will more accurately describe your strengths, but these words can be a good place to start.

Strengths Words

Athletic, Resourceful, Adaptable, Motivated to Achieve, Organized, Initiator, Analytical, Managing, Altruistic, Playful, Ethical, Leader, Communicator, Competitive, Caring, Considerate, Broad perspective, Brave, Observant, Hopeful, Careful, Imaginative, Practical, Sensitive, Mentoring, Strong faith, Appreciative of beauty, Persistent, Disciplined, Authentic, Empathic, Evenhanded, Focused, Goal- Oriented, Curiosity, Socially responsible, Thinks ahead, Articulate, Cooperative, Tolerant, Creative, Kind, Grateful, Trustworthy, Aware of feelings, Honest, Artistic, Sees patterns, Brings people together, Sympathetic, Hospitable, Inquisitive, Cheerful, Intellectual, Self-controlled, Introspective, Follows through, Intelligent, Zestful, Lifetime learner, Inventive, Thrifty, Researching, Charismatic, Efficient, Fair, Open minded, Optimistic, Responsible, Problem solver, Intuitive, Self-confident, Intense, Friendly, Wisdom, Enthusiastic, Balanced, Prudent, Energetic, Generous, Responsible, Even tempered, Enjoys people,

Witty, Courageous, Original, Diplomatic, Loyal, Skilled negotiator, Mechanical, Persuasive, Planner, Coordinating, Foresight, Critical thinker, Humility, Spiritual, Musical, Technical, Spatial, Computing.

List a few positive moments:

1

2

3

My ideas about strengths that might have contributed to making these moments possible.

List a few positive moments:

1

2

3

My ideas about strengths that might have contributed to making these moments possible.

List a few positive moments:

1

2

3

My ideas about strengths that might have contributed to making these moments possible.

List a few positive moments:

1

2

3

My ideas about strengths that might have contributed to making these moments possible.

List a few positive moments:

1

2

3

My ideas about strengths that might have contributed to making these moments possible.

List a few positive moments:

1

2

3

My ideas about strengths that might have contributed to making these moments possible.

List a few positive moments:

1

2

3

My ideas about strengths that might have contributed to making these moments possible.

Morning
What happened? Which part of the experience really felt good? How did I feel?

Afternoon
What happened? Which part of the experience really felt good? How did I feel?

Evening
What happened? Which part of the experience really felt good? How did I feel?

Jennifer Rose, MA

I received my 500-hour yoga teacher certification from the Himalayan Institute, established by Swami Rama. I have been teaching yoga since 2000 and meditation since 2003. I am the founder of the Clear Water Meditation Circle and as well as the moderator of the online teleconference Conversations With the Walking Yogi. Yoga instruction frequently touts the value of a positive mental focus. When I read Jerald Forster's first book, <u>Articulating Strengths Together</u>, I recognized a tool for attaining this positive focus. Jerald and I have worked together to hone his methods into a transformational personal practice. I would encourage anyone who is interested in making his or her thinking process more positive to invest time in learning the SfI-Practice.

Jerald R. Forster, PhD

I graduated from the Counseling Psychology Doctoral Program at the University of Minnesota and became a faculty member of the University of Washington Counseling Psychology program in 1966. I was influenced by the Personal Construct Psychology of George Kelly and the idea that people construct their own realities. It made sense to me in this light to emphasize personal strengths in the construction of a subjective identity. The Strengths-focused Identity (SfI) Practice on this website includes the distillation of my work in psychology. Now, I am most interested in facilitating the optimal development of those who choose to be SfI practitioners.

Made in the USA
Middletown, DE
23 May 2025